# THE MAGIC CANDLE
## by Charmaine Dey

The main object of this book is to help you understand what you are doing, and to create and develop your own techniques and rituals which will surely bring you the results you desire.

It doesn't matter what your religion is. You really don't have to be religious (or anti-religious) at all. Candle burning is a Psychic and Psychological experience, and may compliment your particular faith by arranging your rituals to blend into it. Nevertheless, you need not do anything which you feel is inharmonious with your personal beliefs, as there are countless alternatives.

There are countless authorities and traditions which attempt to tell you precisely what to do in each type of candle-burning ritual or "spell," but few which attempt to explain the reasons why it must be just so. The actual reason is because that is what works best for them — but does it mean anything to you?

The one basic simple fact we can feel sure of is that the act of burning candles does indeed cause an altered state of awareness, producing changes in circumstances. Think of the millions of men and women who have been persuaded and seduced, or extracted promises and proposals, concluded business deals, patched up squabbles, and resolved differences of opinion in the glowing magic of a candlelight supper. And many a birthday wish has come true when all the candles were blown out!

## ORIGINAL PUBLICATIONS

ISBN 0-942272-00-5

$3

# The Magic Candle

## By Charmaine Dey

Facts and Fundamentals of
Ritual Candle Burning

# THE MAGIC CANDLE

## FACTS AND FUNDAMENTALS OF RITUAL CANDLE-BURNING

**by**
**Charmaine Dey**

Original Publications
Division of Jamil Product Corp
2486 Webster Ave.
Bronx, N.Y. 10458

All rights to this book have
been purchased from the author.

ISBN 0-942272-00-5

© 1982 Original Publications

# CONTENTS

# CONTENTS
*(Continued)*

# INTRODUCTION

There are countless authorities and traditions which attempt to tell you precisely what to do in each type of candle-burning ritual or "spell," but few which attempt to explain the reasons why it must be just so. The actual reason is because that is what works best for them — but does it mean anything to you?

The one basic simple fact we can feel sure of is that the act of burning candles does indeed cause an altered state of awareness, producing changes in circumstances. Think of the millions of men and women who have been persuaded and seduced, or extracted promises and proposals, concluded business deals, patched up squabbles, and resolved differences of opinion in the glowing magic of a candlelight supper. And many a birthday wish has come true when all the candles were blown out!

It doesn't matter what your religion is. You really don't have to be religious (or anti-religious) at all. Candle burning is a Psychic and Psychological experience, and may compliment your particular faith by arranging your rituals to blend into it. Nevertheless, you need not do anything which you feel is inharmonious with your personal beliefs, as there are countless alternatives.

The main object of this book is to help you understand what you are doing, and to create and develop your own techniques and rituals which well surely bring you the results you desire.

When the novice enters the local supply shop he is faced with a myriad of strange looking candles of different sizes, shapes and colors — some of them downright frightening in appearance! It is no wonder that the majority of "Good Christians" consider the "entire" Art as "the work of the devil" — Black Magic — Voodoo.

However, when you understand what each of these mysterious objects is intended to represent and how it is used, you will realize that a red nude figure, or a black or green "devil" may be just as innocent as a pink birthday candle — and the skull candles are not simply halloween decorations.

Therefore, our first objective is to acquaint you with the different types, kinds, and colors of candles, and to explain what each is for and how they are generally used.

There are no firm rules as to what must be said or done in each case, in order to effect a successful candle spell. It must mean something to the operator performing it. Some may achieve results by burning a single candle with a purpose firmly in mind.

8

Others may do better with an elaborate ceremony, surrounded by symbols and vested in eloquent robes. It can be as simple or as complicated as you wish to make it. The important thing is to pour a part of yourself into each spell. You will eventually learn to create your own chants, movements, dramatizations, and rituals.

# PART ONE

# TYPES OF CANDLES

Most candles manufactured in the United States are made of Beeswax, parrafin, or stearite, or combinations of these and other good waxes which serve as hardeners, drip-retarders, etc. You will seldom find any made of animal fats as they were in the olden times, so you probably need not inquire as to the composition, as the supplier uses materials in each type of candle best suited to the purpose for which it is designed. There are "straights", tapers, pillars, sculptures, and glass-encased candles which are all used for ritual purposes. The tapers are usually dripless, unless otherwise specified.

There are three main categories into which you can classify the candles used in candle burning rituals. This is not to assume that they must all be used in any spell — nor is the number of candles necessarily limited by "minimum" or "maximum." You may burn one — or 100. But you must understand the basic symbolism of each of them.

The three main classifications of candles used in Spiritual work are: (1) the main Altar or INVOCATIONAL candles, which are lit to summon the presence of a Diety or Special Power; (2) the Personal, or ASTRAL candles which represent individuals; and (3) the Purpose or OFFERTORY candles which carry the petition or desire into the Cosmic.

## ALTAR CANDLES:

There are various different kinds of invocational candles. These are traditionally used during any ritual for Spiritual Protection. They are usually dressed and dedicated to a special Diety (ies). The act of lighting them serves to call upon the presence of that (or those) Diety (ies). When they are extinguished, the Diety (ies) are thereby dismissed.

Altar candles may be re-used in various rituals, until they are no longer attractive, or until they are too small to be dignified alongside of the other candles in the ritual. If you choose to use them at all, be certain that they are predominant — by their size, positioning on the altar, etc.

Your Altar candles should be of a size larger than the others. If you are using small 3/4" candles in the ritual, then select a pair of 1 1/4" thick "jumbo" candles, or two tall, majestic tapers for your Altar. If you are burning 7-day glass-enclosed candles for your ritual, you might choose a 14-day glass-enclosed for the altar, so that you can be certain the altar candle will not go out before your petition candle burns out. Some may prefer to just use a 7-day with a particular Saint's picture on it. It is advisable to keep a spare on hand, just in case the Saint candle burns faster than the petition candle so the new one can be lit from the old before it goes out.

Very popular are the Cruciform candles, some bearing a rose at the center, others with "keys of wisdom" inscribed upon them. Whatever type you use, if any, they should give you a feeling of Spiritual security. Experiment — with, and without. Find out what works best for you.

The colors for your Altar candles may be all white, all gold, different colors for the days of the week, or the seasons of the year. Here are the traditional colors in the latter cases:

Sunday (Sun) — Gold
Monday (Moon) — Silver or grey
Tuesday (Mars) — Red
Wednesday (Mercury) — Yellow
Thursday (Jupiter) — Bright Blue
Friday (Venus) — Green
Saturday (Saturn) — Purple

These serve to invoke the special planetary influences designated by each "Power" or "God", which will be described in a later chapter.

Spring (The Water element) — Green
Summer (The Fire element) — Red
Autumn (The Air element) — Yellow
Winter (The Earth element) — Blue

These serve to focus energies on the special area symbolized by each of the four elements: Water — the emotions; Fire — the Spirit; Air — the intellect; Earth — material things.

People of the Pagan Faith like to burn one white and one black candle, symbolizing the Heavenly Father and the Earth Mother — masculine and feminine aspects of the Supreme Being. Those who have qualms about a black candle may prefer to use one gold and one silver. The only steadfast rule to observe is: "Do whatever TURNS YOU ON!"

There are many who choose to devote a small corner or niche in their home to a permanent Altar of some kind. This may be a Temple, or a Shrine to a favorite Diety or Saint, or simply a peaceful, hallowed place to which one may retreat in daily joys and sorrows for prayer, devotion or thanksgiving.

It is customary in these cases to keep a "perpetual flame" burning on the Altar, from which all additional candles may be lit. This is called the "Sanctum Lamp", and is usually a 7-day Vigil candle of white or natural wax encased in colored glass. It is replaced each week, the new one being lit from the old just before it goes out.

The color of the glass may be selected symbolically according to one's needs: Red for protection against harm; green for health and abundance; Blue for Peace and Devotion; Gold for purification or Success; Rose for love and happiness.

Or, if a statue is placed upon the Shrine or Altar, the color may compliment the Diety, or Saint to whom the Altar is dedicated, for instance; Red for Christ, St. Barbara, St. Michael, etc.; Blue for the Blessed Mother in her many manifestations; Green for St. Jude...etc.

AN ANCIENT CUSTOM: The flame on the original Vigil candle is often lit by a process known as "Drawing Down the Sun." An altar charcoal is ignited by using a magnifying glass in the sun, focusing the glass to hold a beam of light on the charcoal until it is ignited. Then a bit of Sandalwood powder or chips, or other sacred woods are added with a pinch of saltpetre to speed up the process. When a flame appears, the candle is lit from it with a taper or lighting stick.

This procedure is renewed once each year, usually on the Thursday before Easter (Maundy Thursday), or at the Vernal Equinox, and a fresh candle is lit from the "new fire." In the event the Perpetual Flame should accidentally be extinguished, it may be renewed again by "drawing down the Sun," preferably on a Sunday However, if it happens to be a rainy or overcast season, a sunbeam must be captured whenever possible. This is often quite an inconvenience, so if you keep a Sacred Flame, guard it with care — and purchase a good brand of candles which are likely to remain lit!

## ASTRAL CANDLES:

The second classification consists of what are usually referred to as "Astral" candles, the word "Astral" meaning "starry", or "star-like." These are used to represent the person who is burning the candles, or the person(s) for whom the candles are being burned. Therefore, the name implies that each individual is like a star in the universe.

These may be of any size, but must burn throughout the entire ritual along with the "purpose" candle. Some may choose to burn a "Zodiac" candle bearing their personal sign. Others may like a large "pillar" type candle which may be used time and again, but must not be larger or more predominant than any Altar candles use.

If you are using 3/4" diameter straight candles, or "jumbo" pillar candles for your petitions, then you may use Astral candles of the same size, discarding the remnants with each spell. It is also popular to use the tapered type for Astral candles, as they often come in a wider array of colors from which to select. They may be re-used or discarded each time, as you desire, however the only rule to observe is that they may never be used to represent a different individual — only the person for whom they were originally dedicated.

If you are burning a 7-day glass enclosed "Novena" candle for your petition, you may use a 7-day glass enclosed candle for your Astral. These are available in plain, clear glass with colored waxes. You may place a picture of yourself, or the person whom the candle represents on, or in front of it, or paint initials, Zodiac signs, etc. on the glass with red nail polish.

The colors of the Astral candles must be representative of **you**, or the persons included in your petition. If you are doing the work for someone else, you must select the color for that person, just as though you were painting a picture to be hung in his or her home.

"Astral colors" may mean your Zodiac color (or colors), or may mean simply colors which make you "feel" good. The latter seem to work best. You might get a hint by inspecting your wardrobe and your environment. Do you find that nearly everything you own is some shade of blue? Then select a blue Astral candle for yourself. Is your friend's apartment done all in shades of yellows and oranges? Then try a gold Astral candle for that person...etc. Perhaps you are changeable, like most people. Keep a supply of **all** your favorite colors, and match your current mood! Just remember that in the ritual, the candle IS YOU (or "the girl in the green dress," "the Scorpio man", or "the red-haired person,"...etc.

It is customary to inscribe the person's initials or zodiac symbol on the Astral candle at the time it is dressed and dedicated. If neither of these is known, some other means of identification may be used, such as "O.W." (other woman)..."N.N." (nosy neighbor)..."J" (Judge)...etc.

## PETITION (OFFERTORY) CANDLES:

This third category includes all the different kinds of candles which may be burned to represent the **purpose** of the ritual.

It is possible to achieve excellent results by using one or more candles in this category only, without the use of Altar or Astral candles. The other two groups add majesty and symbolism to any spell, but are actually embellishments which the ritual-worker will add as he or she becomes more involved in the Art.

The Petition candle may be any size, shape, or form, including plain candles of the proper color, specially-molded or carved figurines such as "Adam and Eve" (nude male and female figures), Black cats, 7-knobbed, serpents, skulls, symbolic fruits ("Love apple", an ear of corn to represent abundance, etc)...or, they may be small colored votive candles placed in a glass jar.

Very popular is the "Novena" candle, which may be 3, 7, 9, or 14-day glass enclosed, and decorated with symbols, pictures, and prayers declaring the purpose for the ritual.

The word "Novena" is Latin, meaning "A New Beginning." However, the custom originated way back in Ancient Egypt, and has been world-wide in its use. The idea is to "burn away" all the old troubles, or mistakes, and begin anew, with a clean, unobstructed viewpoint. The Novena is therefore **best** begun at the New Moon for Spiritual Strengthening — following which, positive results may be expected within a week, if proper thought has been poured into it.

The glass-enclosed Novena candle must never be extinguished once it has been lit. It must remain burning until it burns out by itself. So if you use this type of ritual, be certain that you have a place where you may leave it in safety. A good suggestion is to place it in a metal pie or cake pan, in case the glass should crack (which doesn't happen too often, but it is possible). The melted liquid wax will then go into the pan, not all over your dresser or coffee table, and is less likely to catch on fire.

Devote a few minutes each day or evening to a quiet prayer or meditation, concentrating upon your request or problem.

In many parts of the world, the "Novena" is performed as a 9-day ritual, begun at the Last Quarter (waning) Moon's phase, and running into the First Quarter (waxing) phase. Nine small candles are burned, one each day. They may be short, colored candles which burn away in two or three hours, or the small "votive" lights which are burned in a glass jar, and may be purchased in either 10 or 15-hour types. These are allowed to burn completely out, replacing them the following day with a fresh one. The ritual should begin promptly at the same appointed hour each day, with the first 10 or 15 minutes devoted to heavy concentration. *t m p*

Many people prefer the plain colored "jumbo" or pillar type of candle. The broader the diameter, the longer it will last — however they are not intended to be left burning for any length of time, especially unattended, for they will form a "well" of liquid wax. Then if the heat causes one wall to collapse, the liquid will run out all over the surroundings, and even may cause danger of fire. Candles over 1 1/2" in diameter are not very economical, as they will need to be trimmed of the "hollow" portion left when the flame burns down the center, and most of the candle is wasted.

The best way to use the jumbo candle is to mark it into portions, for as many days as you want the ritual to run. Then each day when that section has been burned, extinguish it with a snuffer, or blow it out. *IMP*

For very difficult problems, the jumbo candle is used by many ritualists with 15 to 20-minute meditation or chanting sessions, on successive days, or at each of a certain planetary hour — that is, once each seven hours. The candle is extinguished when the power to hold a "thought-form" or visualization diminishes or is broken. Astral and Altar candles are lit and extinguished at the same times in each case.

## NOVELTY CANDLES:

**THE 7-KNOBBED CANDLE.** Very popular among ritualists is the candle molded into seven "knobs", or "knots." The idea is to burn one knob each day to bring about a special wish, or un-do an undesirable situation, thereby eliminating one obstacle in the way of fulfillment at each sitting. In this case, each day's session should be at the same hour. Choose a time when least likely to be disturbed, and concentrate upon your wish as long as you are able to hold a strong visualization in your mind. *tmp*

In some places these candles are only available in one or two colors, (such as black or red.) In this event, use the black for any "banishing" purpose, and the red for any "activating" purpose, such as a wish. *jmp*

However, if you have a variety of colors from which to choose, following are some of the special uses to which you might apply them:

If someone is witholding money that rightfully is yours, or if your property is being tied up with restraining orders or litigation, burn a green 7-knob candle.

If someone has a "hold" upon you, or you suspect you are the victim of a sortilege "binding" spell worked on you by an unwanted lover — burn a black 7-knob candle.

If someone is tying up or delaying your law suit, and you wish to have your day in court, burn a brown 7-knob candle.

To eliminate obstacles in the path of your love, burn a red 7-knob candle.

To remove bad luck which may have been plaguing you, burn a yellow 7-knob.

To remove a hex or psychic attack, or to eliminate various minor health problems, burn a purple 7-knob.

To eliminate depression, squabbling and confusion, burn a blue 7-knob.

For a secret wish to come true, burn a white 7-knob candle.

To eliminate obstacles in the way of business success and career, burn an orange 7-knob.

If you cannot obtain the 7-knob candles, or prefer the glass-enclosed type, an alternate way to achieve the same results is to burn a 7-colored, 7-day novena candle. One color will usually burn away each day, focusing upon each area of life which might be hindered or stifled.

**THE "DOUBLE-ACTION" OR "REVERSING" CANDLE.** These are jumbo-type candles of white, red or green, with the lower half hand-dipped in a coating of black. They are designed to "reverse" the actions of any evil worked against you by another person. The white and black are used to reverse another's bad spell or hex, the red and black for cases where someone is destroying your love life, and the green and black for instances when someone is causing you money problems and bankruptcy.

18

The symbolism dramatized by the burning of this type of candle is as follows: The colored candle represents the desired circumstance, while the black coating represents the undesired influences being perpetrated against the individual, and "pulling him down." As the clear (undipped) portion burns, it drips **over** the offending portion, "trapping" and neutralizing it, or "overcoming" the situation. It is assumed that if a person's "evil" or magic misses its mark, it will **reverse**, and return to its sender.

Here is an example of how the Double-Action candle might be used. If you feel that you are the victim of someone's "evil-eye", or vicious rumors and gossip, dress a black and white double-action candle and, with an iron or steel nail, inscribe an eye in a triangle on the upper (white) portion. Then stick the nail in the candle at the half-way mark, between the white and black portions. Set the candle up on a reflective surface such as foil or a mirror. Burn the candle on a Tuesday soon after the full moon.

If some third party is jealously trying to break up your love affair or marriage, use a red and black candle, and inscribe two hearts, with the initials of you and your lover on the upper (red) portion. Follow the same procedure as in the previous, except burn the candle on a Friday, with the moon waxing.

In the event a jealous competitor is hurting your business with unfair practices, or a vicious tongue, use a green and black candle. Follow the same basic procedure, only inscribe dollar signs and money symbols on the green portion of the candle, with your own initials. You may put the initials of the competitor on the lower half (black). Burn on a Saturday with the Moon waxing.

When each of the spells has been completed, and the candle has burned completely out, wrap all remains — drippings, with the nail, etc., in the foil, or scrape it from the mirror, and wrap in waxed paper or parchment, then bury it. Include the ashes from any incense you have burned during the ritual.

**THE "SEPARATION" CANDLE.** This is a red Jumbo candle which has been hand-dipped in a coating of black — covering the entire candle. The red candle symbolizes the person whom you wish to be liberated or freed from the bondage or enchantment of an undesirable mate or partner.

This book is not intended to advise you as to what is right and what is wrong, but simply to tell you how these things are traditionally done. It is up to you to decide whether what you are doing is an innocent effort to help someone, or whether it might bring harm upon another.

Very often a mother will be tormented by a son helplessly in love with some prostitute, or trifling woman who squanders his life's earnings recklessly, and is throwing him upon the mercy of the shylocks. Or perhaps a daughter is married to a brute who beats and injures her and the children, and drinks up every penny so that the daughter is utterly poverty-stricken, and too black and blue to get a job on her own. One can very easily see that in cases of this kind it would be quite a blessing to break them up if possible. Or, if your husband is being cheated by his business partner, you might like to see the partnership dissolved.

Nevertheless, as the candle burns, you can "see" the object of the spell being gradually freed of the "bondage" represented by the outer layer melting off or being covered over by drippings from the inner candle.

Available in some places, or often prepared at home, is another kind of "break-up" candle, said to be very powerful in breaking up a marriage or love-affair. It is a straight candle with a coiled serpent upon it. The serpent symbolizes the one who has the other party in their clutches, or the "tempter" who is leading the innocent one astray. It works in much the same way as the Separation candle, however is usually quite a bit more costly as it is difficult to make.

**IMAGE CANDLES.** These are little nude figurines of men and women, and come in a variety of colors for different purposes. The most popular are the red and the black ones. It is mistakenly believed that these little effigies are strictly "Voo-Doo", and relegated to the Black Arts. But there is evidence that the practice of burning wax images for all sorts of purposes is wide spread throughout the world. Most authorities claim that the custom originated in Scotland, but there is historical documentation that the practice was very popular in ancient Egypt and Babylonia as well as other Pagan countries.

Nevertheless, many a maiden has nailed her man through the working of red image candles, which have been popularly re-named "Love" candles, or "Adam and Eve" candles. Likewise many a man has captured his lady love through the working of this type of candle magic.

They can also be used for "banishing", or getting rid of an undesirable lover, or other person, or to bring about healing by banishing an illness. They are often used to separate two *Peter* parties, while at the same time drawing the one you love closer *White* to yourself. This is the most popular kind of candle burning in cases where someone has stolen a husband, wife or lover, and the victim wants to have him or her return home.

The candles are set up and moved about upon the altar, according to whether you wish to draw two people closer together, or have them drift apart. In the event you wish to draw them together, the two candles representing the couple are set up about a foot or so apart, facing each other. At each day's session, they are gently moved about an inch or so closer together, until the two candles are as close together as they can get.

In the event you wish to have two people drift apart from each other, set the candles up close together, turned back to back. At each day's session move them an inch or so farther apart, until they are as far from each other as your space will allow.

There are many cases wherein the operator wishes to have someone leave the party they are with, and come to themself, (or to the one for whom they are casting the spell.) In this instance three candles are used, one to represent each of the parties — the couple as they are presently, and the one who wishes to put them asunder and capture the one they love for themself. The "couple" are set up back to back on one side of the altar, with the desired lover on the inside, and the unwanted partner on the outside. The person who wishes to attract the lover is placed on the opposite side of the altar, facing the lover. Then, each day the two which are facing each other are moved gradually together, leaving the third candle remaining in its place. This arrangement clearly dramatizes the desired situation.

One way to use the Image Candle for healing is as follows: You will need one male or female Image candle to represent the person who is afflicted, and a pair of Altar candles. Some people like to include a picture or statue of a particular Diety or Saint to whom they wish to make an appeal for help in healing the individual. However, this is not mandatory, and you may prefer to "send" your own powers of healing directly to the person. The Image candle is laid upon its back on the altar, simulating a person lying inert in bed. On the first day, you light **only** the Altar candles, and as you pray or meditate upon healing the individual, you anoint the Image candle with healing oil — stroking it gently as you visualize strength and new life entering the body. When you are finished with your meditation session for the day, extinguish the Altar candles and cover the Image candle with a clean handkerchief or cloth.

On the second day, the Image candle is stood up on its "feet," facing the Altar — that is, looking **toward** the "Powers that be," rather than **away** from them. Again, only the Altar candles are lit, and you spend the session meditating on the healing taking place, while gently stroking the Image candle with the healing oil. After the session, extinguish the Altar candles, lay the Image candle down in a sleeping position again, and cover it up.

On the third day, the Image candle is stood up, only this time, (after lighting the Altar candles) the Image candle is lit. Now you must begin to visualize the illness **leaving** the body, and the strength of the Spirit glowing within — filling all the tissues with new vitality, and destroying any foreign matter which is impairing the health. When you are no longer able to concentrate, extinguish the Image candle by carefully blowing it out, while you think of banishing the illness. Then take the candle in your hands and wash it in a dish of clean water. Anoint it with the healing oil, extinguish the Altar candles, lay the Image candle on its back and cover it. This process should be repeated each day until the Image candle is completely burned out — allowing it to burn out on the final day when it is just an unrecognizable "stump."

Perhaps these examples have helped you to grasp the general idea, which is to "act out" the situation as you desire it to be. You must use your imagination, and create your own specialized rituals to fit each situation. Watch a small child playing with dollies, and you will catch on quickly!

When you are finished with each ritual, the drippings and remnants of the candles must be gathered up in a clean sheet of paper, and properly disposed of by burying. This, as you will later learn, is because the candles have been blessed and anointed, and any sacred, consecrated object must never be desecrated by throwing it in a garbage heap or trash pile.

**BLACK CAT CANDLES.** Many people believe that burning a candle in the form of a black cat will banish bad luck, so that good luck may come their way. However, if you are among those to whom a black cat represents **good** luck rather than bad, it would be better to use some alternate method.

**SKULL CANDLES.** One of the most commonly used rituals in cases of very serious or terminal illness, is to burn a

Skull-shaped candle to banish "impending death." It is accompanied by an Astral candle of the appropriate color, which must be a size which will burn as long as, or longer than the Skull candle. The Astral candle represents the person, and the Skull represents "Death."

They are placed side-by-side upon the altar, then moved gradually **away** from each other, moving them an inch or so at each day's sitting, or prayer session as you concentrate upon health and vitality flooding the person. "Death" moves away, and his face diminishes. It is claimed that if the Skull candle happens to burn away on the **inside** only, leaving the external form intact — the threat remains, and you must repeat the ritual, putting more power into it.

**SATAN CANDLES.** These are also called "Devil-be-gone" candles, and are molded in the shape of "the evil one." They are burned in exorcisms, and in instances when someone feels they are being tormented by the Devil, or their house is infested with evil vibrations. The idea is, of course, that as the candle burns and diminishes, the Devil is being banished. If you feel that a particular person is possessed by the Devil, and wish to free him of this obsession, burn the Devil candle with an Astral candle to represent the person. Be certain that the Astral candle is large enough to out-last the Devil candle. They may be moved gradually apart from each other at each day's session, just as described for the Image and Skull candle rituals.

**THE TRIPLE-ACTION CANDLE.** Another way to rid an environment, or a person of destructive influences, commonly referred to as a "crossed condition," is to burn a three-colored candle (usually red, white, and blue, or, popular among Latin Americans is red, white and green.) They are believed to release the highest Spiritual vibrations, banishing the bad or unhealthy influences. They may be burned alone, or with an Astral candle to represent an individual.

The symbolism of three colors may represent "The Holy Trinity," or "Health, Purity and Peace," (red white and blue), "Health, Peace, and Prosperity," (red white and green) etc. Many think of the red white and blue as "Love, Truth, and Friendship." These candles are often burned in the home to bring good luck in general, or to bring peace into a quarrelsome atmosphere.

**MEMORIAL CANDLES.** The traditional Memorial candle is a 24 to 30-hour candle of pure white or naturlal wax, contained in a white or colored votive glass about the size of a water tumbler. It may be plain, or have prayers printed upon it. This is generally lit at midnight or sunrise, to inaugurate a day of remembrance dedicated to a special holiday, birthday, or anniversary. Many light them at the vesper hour to commemorate the passing of a dear one.

CRUCIFORM ALTAR CANDLES

Sanctum Lamp

7 Day Novena Candles
in glass

14 Day

# COLOR SYMBOLISM

The color of a candle (or of anything in your immediate environment) is like a "key" which unlocks a certain compartment of your sub-conscious mind, and of your entire being. Those who cannot actually "see" colors can nevertheless feel their vibratory effects, because **pigment** is **matter** releasing energy at a certain rate of speed, or "wave-length." That wave-length, or frequency activates, or energizes a certain part of your being as it penetrates your sight or your aura. Its impulses are transmitted to your brain along the nerve routes.

Each color carries the vibratory effects of one of the Planetary influences, and/or one of the four "elements," — Earth, Fire, Air, or Water.

The actual symbolization of each color will be found to differ with authority, tradition, or school of thought, and in the final analysis, the only actual true authority for **you** is yourself!

However, if you are not quite sure what each color means to you, or "reminds you of," or "Makes you feel like," here are some universal guidelines from the fields of pyschology, art and religion, which you may or may not accept:

## BLACK

This is the most controversial of all. We will try to represent both aspects of the controversy, and you must decide for yourself.

There are those who feel that Black is "evil", and disparage the thought of ever burning any kind of black candle in the fear that it "releases" all sorts of bad or dangerous influences. If you have been previously conditioned to this type of belief, it is probably best that you follow your own intuition about it, because it is **your** sub-conscious mind with which you are dealing in your selection.

For those with a more open attitude, who have not been so conditioned, there is a completely different, and more scientific side of the story.

Black is the **absence** or **void** of any and all coloring, therefore it does not radiate or emit any vibration of its own at all! As a matter of fact, being void, it is of female/negative polarity — absorbing rather than emitting any energy. Then, as it burns, it "releases" only that which has been placed into or upon it. So, how **you** have charged it determines whether it is "good" or "evil." Always be certain to prepare the candle carefully prior to burning it, observing the ritual of cleansing and exorcism to thoroughly remove any impressions previously placed on it through manufacture and handling in the store.

Black represents the "still of the night," inertia, the deep cold and tranquil waters — the deepest recesses of the unconscious mind. A burning black candle symbolizes "light coming out of the darkness."

Therefore, since it does not exert any interfering energies of its own, it is a fine choice for meditation purposes, and psychic development. Many like to burn a black candle when they are requesting something of a "miraculous" nature — that is, a **joyous** outcome to a grim or impossible situation. There is hardly a better choice, or a suitable substitute in banishing rituals of the most serious type.

### WHITE
White is the **balanced** presence of **all** colors in synthesis. It therefore gives off a very positive and powerful vibration. White can be used as a substitute for **any** color if what you want is unavailable at the time. So keep well stocked with white candles for emergencies.

White traditionally sumbolizes Purity, Truth, Sincerity, Virtue of all kinds, and the highest Spirituality.

### RED
Red is the color of life's blood, and emits a very strong, positive vibration. It is "fiery," and the intense shades are extremely Martian in character. The Red influence incites (or excites) **Passion**, whether it be for love, sex acquisition, an intense desire of any sort, courage, energy, strength, and radiant health. Red candles are often burned for protection against any psychic attack, physical harm inflicted through Black Magic performed by enemies, and to conquer fear or laziness.

### PINK
Pink is a color which generates affection, self-generosity, belflessness. It is an excellent choice for matters of domestic, or "true" love, as it symbolizes Love, Honor, Togetherness, Gentleness, and Spiritual fulfillment. Pink candles may be burned for some healings, especially of the **spirit**. Vivid, deep pinks help to "break up" bad prevailing conditions of many kinds, as they certainly dispel gloom and negativity. "Hot Pink" is a color of great joy and sensual pleasure.

## ORANGE

Orange is closely akin to the Sun of midsummer. It is therefore a color of great **power**. It symbolizes enthusiasm, fun, vitality, stimulation, adaptability, attraction, and friendship. It is burned for success, and also to draw or attract good things and friendly people.

## GOLD

Gold symbolizes Universal Fraternity, great fortune, the intuitive faculties, and the "Cosmic mind." It can be burned to promote understanding, for Divinatory rituals, and to bring about Peace in a community or group. Gold candles are also used to bring fast luck insofar as financial benefits are concerned, when the obstacles seem to exist outside of your immediate control — for instance, if you wish to attract a buyer for something, or would like to see your stock go up.

## YELLOW

Yellow is the color of the Air element (which governs mental activity,) and its radiations stimulate the intellect and imagination. It symbolizes Adaptiveness, Creativity, Skills, Commerce, Medicine, Diplomacy, Counselling, and **sudden changes.**

Yellow candles are burned in operations aimed at "bending the mind" of another. Also to aid the memory, for healing, to improve business, and for success in the performing arts. It is also good to promote cheerfulness in a perpetual grouch. Many people of the Carribbean traditions also burn yellow to chase '"evil," and for exorcism.

## GREEN

Green is the color of the Venus planetary influence, and also of the productive meadows of the Earth. It therefore symbolizes Nature, and Material gain, Fertility, Abundance, Good Fortune, Cooperation, Generosity, Good Health, and Renewal.

Green candles are burned to gain money, to bring abundance of any kind, or to bring about matrimony. Also to retain or regain a youthful appearance; to "loosen up" a skinflint; also to promote balance and harmony in any off-balance situation. Green is also used in any circumstance requiring a fresh, healthier outlook, or a repeat or renewal of a spell in order to perpetuate it, or protect it from deterioration.

## BLUE

**Light** blue is the color of devotion and inspiration. It traditionally represents Peace and Blessings in the home, immortality, Tranquility, and Masculine Youth or Innocence. Light blue is often used by women to keep a man "faithful," to retain a son's love in spite of a hostile influence, etc. Hence the term "true blue."

Deeper, vivid **Royal** blue is the color of the Jupiter planetary influence, and represents laughter and joviality, Loyalty on a communal level, successful group enterprise, and **expansion**. Study the effects of the Jupiter influence carefully before electing to invoke this power, as there are many misconceptions over this controversial planet. It is one power which can easily run amok if not properly used.

### PURPLE

Purple is the color of Sovereignty or Royalty, Dignity, Wisdom, Idealism, Psychic manifestation, and Spirit contact. Therefore it is used when great Spiritual power is necessary.

Purple is effectively used against Black Magic, demoniac possession (to drive away evil,) to break up a "jinxed" condition, and for Spiritual or Psychic healing. It is also used to throw up a veil of Spiritual protection.

### INDIGO

Candles of such a dark hue that they are closely akin to black, but actually a purplish-blue, are the color of the Saturn planetary influence, and used primarily to promote **inertia**.

They are an excellent choice for deep meditation, as they tend to still the mind of any mental activity.

They are popularly burned in spells wherein you wish to halt the actions of someone — to stop gossip, lies, undersirable competition, or to neutralize another's magic.

Indigo is also used to expedite Karma, or for "repentence," leaving a clearer insight and wisdom gained by experience.

### MAGENTA

This color is rarely mentioned in most candle burning books, becuase it is often difficult to find — being available usually only in the dinner taper, and pillar types, and available mostly in places where candles are sold primarily for their ornamental value.

But they are really worth trying to find, and if you should — **stock up**, becuase they may not have them the next time you want one.

28

Magenta is not a color of the spectrum, but actually an illusionary "oscillation," between the infra-red and ultra-violet bands, vibrating at a very high frequency. It is an actinic, penetrating color, and denotes **Super Power.** This "color" is named for the Magi, and literally means "Magic Color."

It will penetrate all planes, is etheric in nature, and has the tendency to work **fast.**

Magenta may be burned with other colored candles to promote speedy action, or by itself to expedite a lagging result.

It is positively the best color for Spiritual Healing, Exorcisms and quick changes of a favorable nature.

But be certain that it is a clean, vibrant hue, preferably flourescent if you can obtain it. The less vibrant shades tend to exert a decidedly Scorpio influence, which may or may not be what you want.

Magenta symbolizes OMNIPOTENCE.

### SILVER [or Light Gray]
This is traditionally the color of Stability and Neutrality. Candles of this color are burned to remove evil influences, or to neutralize any existing undesirable vibrations.

Silver candles used with meditation help to aid the development of psychic abilities and ESP.

Metallic silver Altar candles can be used to invoke the assistance of The Great Mother, or Goddess aspect of Diety.

### BROWN
Brown is the color of the soil — Earth, and its vibration is concentrated in the material plane.

Some people like to burn brown candles in time of financial crises, as it allegedly attracts money and financial success.

Brown Altar candles may be used on occasions, to attract the Earth Spirits, who must always be remunerated for their aid, and properly dismissed, or returned to the Earth with a special Ritual. Many will toss a penny into the hole, when they bury the drippings and remnants of the spell. Others like to place special "gifts" upon the Altar, some traditions listing a large pantheon of Spirits, and each one requiring a special gift (such as a cigar, a glass of whiskey, a flower, an ear of corn...etc.) These gifts are buried, of course, with the remnants of the spell.

# "DRESSING" OF CANDLES

Before a candle may be placed upon your Altar, or lit for ritual, it **must** be properly prepared.

"Dressing" a candle consists of three important steps: Cleansing and exorcising it of any previous impressions that may be embedded in it; Blessing the candle; or "Consecrating" it for Spiritual use; and finally, Anointing, or "charging" the candle with your special intentions.

This may seem like a lot of trouble, but successful ritualists wouldn't dream of taking an often-handled candle from a store shelf, placing it on their Altar and lighting it without proper dressing.

### THE CLEANSING

Most purchased or stored candles will be ladened with dust and dirt particles, even if they are factory-wrapped. Some, like those enclosed in glass, will be rather messy with wax drippings from the factory, and a collection of dust and even perhaps insects, from the warehouse. These all have to first be removed, leaving you with a **physically** clean article. Also, Altar candles which have been used until they are thick and distorted with drippings, or been left standing out on an open Altar for some time, will need to be cleaned up and trimmed off to burn evenly. Some types of molded or carved figure-candles may be imperfect, or "lop-sided" at the base, etc. These will have to be trimmed up to make them more suitable.

You will need a clean working area (other than your Altar) upon which is a clean sheet of paper. Waxed kitchen paper will serve fine, or paper towels. If you are cleaning up used Altar candles, you will need an additional sheet or two of clean white paper in which to collect all of the used drippings for proper disposal to the elements. Remember, these have been consecrated, and must be handled respectfully.

You will need a small work-knife — preferably one which has been blessed, and which you keep exclusively for this work. It need not be an expensive ritual knife — just a simple little kitchen paring knife, or a folding pocket knife will do beautifully. You will also need some mineral or baby oil. If you have neither, a lemon-scented furniture polish will do very well, since it is only scented mineral oil, and the lemon oil contained in it has excellent cleansing properties. Cleaning or detergent waxes work fine for the purpose also.

You will also require a bit of alcohol or energine to clean any dirty looking wicks, and some clean soft cloths of cotton, linen, muslin, or flannel.

With the knife, trim away any unwanted wax from the candle(s). Also, if you wish to do any additional carving of any kind, this is the proper time to do it. Next, pour some of the oil or detergent on the clean cloth and rub off any soil that is on the candle(s). If you are using a spray-on type cleaner, it is alright to spray it directly onto the candle, then, when it "lifts" the soil, wipe it dry with a little alcohol or dry cleaning fluid.

Allow the candle(s) to sit for a few minutes until they are completely dry. Sometimes you may wish to take a dry polishing cloth and buff or rub the candles to a nice luster, if they appear dull or hazy. Now they are ready to be moved to the Altar.

## THE EXORCISM AND BLESSING
Place a clean piece of waxed or parchment paper upon the Altar, and set or lay the candle(s) upon it. Do not put them into any holders at this time.

Also upon your Altar you will need: One or more Altar candles; a small bell; incense and burner; some sprinkling water (which may be pure rain or spring water, prepared Holy Water, flower waters such as Rose, Violet, Lilac, Orange Flower, etc., or an eau de cologne such as Florida Water.) You will also require a Sacred Anointing Oil such as Frankincense and Myrr, Jasmine, or an all-purpose blend of Holy Oils. Some prefer unscented Olive Oil, which has been blessed and consecrated for Altar use. In addition, you should now select the Occult Oil which will serve as a fluid condenser in the process of "charging" or loading your candle(s). You may need several different types if you are fixing more than one candle. Place this or these upon the Altar. You will also need the blessed knife, so lay it on the Altar. You are then ready to proceed:

## RITUAL

(Begin with clean body and hands, and clean garments.):

1. Light Altar candle(s) and some good quality Spiritual incense. Sound the bell three times. Say: "Most Holy Spirit, Protector, Consoler, Healer. . . descend upon this Altar and give forth of your Divine Light. Fill this place with Love, the sustaining force of the Universe. Blessed be."

31

2. Make a gesture of Power (this may be the sign of the Solar Cross, or Banishing Pentagram) over the candle(s), and sprinkle with the water while saying: "Let these creatures of wax be **cleansed** (+ or ★ ) and **sanctified** (+ or ★ ) and **blessed** (+ or ★ ) for my intended purpose. May they bring realization of that purpose to the one for whom they shall burn...by all the Powers that be, by and through my hand. Blessed be."

3. Lift the censer, and thoroughly incense the candle(s), saying: "May the petitions and prayers that accompany these candles as they burn, ascend...as does the smoke from this incense...purified and pleasing to the Gods, and mingle with the Holy Cosmic Mind, which knows how to provide for our needs. So be it!"

4. With the blessed knife, cut a Solar Cross or Pentagram into the wax of each candle. For 7-day glass enclosed Novena candles, this will naturally be in the top. For other types, it should be at the base.

5. With your thumb dipped into the Altar Oil, re-trace the symbols, saying: "Be anointed, and dedicated only to the intended purpose. With this oil I seal within thee the sweet essense of Life...that thou may vibrate as a living entity, carrying forth my desires to the Gods. So be it!"

Then ratify this consecration by making the sign of the Solar Cross or **Invoking** Pentagram in the air over the candles.

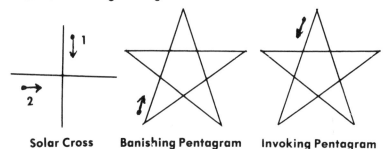

Solar Cross          Banishing Pentagram     Invoking Pentagram

## "CHARGING" THE CANDLES

This procedure consists of rubbing the candle in a certain manner, while concentrating deeply on your purpose or petition, and strongly visualizing the desired outcome. The medium of transferance, via which you will impress those thoughts into the candle, is your Occult Oil, chosen for each individual purpose.

Some may prefer to use a single "candle-dressing" oil on all candles. But it would seem that a product which has been specially formulated from substances of the Planetary and Elemental categories especially suited to the influence desired in each case, would be superior to an all-purpose substance. It is reasonable to assume that your powers of concentration are not equally keen at all times. Therefore, a **previously** "charged" oil, or one which vibrates on a particular wave-length would surely serve to boost these powers, or reinforce them. Also, some types of oils are best for banishing, others for attraction, or drawing. An all-purpose oil would have to be neutral.

It is advised to burn an incense of the same type as your oil during this porcedure, to aid concentration.

The method of rubbing the candle will differ with each different type and purpose. This is the most important operation in your candle burning ritual, and must not be done casually or swiftly.

**FOR GLASS-ENCLOSED CANDLES:** Pour a few drops of the oil into the candle jar. With the first two fingers, rub the oil into the wax. If the candle is for **banishing** purposes, rub in a **clockwise** (deosil) circular direction. If the purpose is to **attract** or draw something closer to you, rub in a    **counter-clockwise** (widdershins) circular direction. Concentrate your thoughts on the desired outcome. Continue the operation until you can no longer hold the thought-picture in mind. Finish by sealing the candle with a Solar Cross or Pentagram drawn on the glass with the fore-finger dipped in the oil.

Wipe hands clean of the oil on a paper or linen towel. If you are doing several candles with different types of oils, clean the hands between operations with a cloth saturated in rubbing alcohol, or one of the sprinkling waters.

**FOR PLAIN WAX CANDLES:** If the purpose of the candle is to **banish** something, for instance, to drive away undesirable influences or conditions, or to get rid of an illness, etc. . . begin by rubbing the candle from the center toward the bottom. Then rub from the center toward the top. (The oil is poured into the hand, not directly onto the candle.) Concentrate deeply on the desired outcome, and be sure to hold a clear picture in the mind of the event happening as you wish it.

For purposes of a **drawing** nature, for instance, to attract a lover to you, to obtain money or property, etc., begin by rubbing the candle from the bottom toward the center, then from the top to the center. Hold your thought-pictures throughout the procedure. In each case, seal the candle with the sign of the Solar Cross or Pentagram drawn in the air over the candles, with the words, "So mote it be!"

**FOR ASTRAL OR IMAGE CANDLES**, representing yourself, or other persons: The directions for rubbing the candles will follow the same rules as for straight candles, but the concentration should be along these lines: "Here stands the image of (me, "George," "Mary," etc.) It thinks as I think, moves as I wish it to move, behaves as I wish it to behave. . .and by my hand **lives** as the true person." At this point, hold the candle up to your mouth and breathe upon it, saying: "Breathe now (name of person) and receive the gift of the Spirit." In some cases it may be, "Breathe now, and receive the gift of life — feel the blessing of vibrant health radiating upon you. . .etc."

**FOR 7-KNOBBED CANDLES:** The candle is rubbed in **one** direction only. If it is to **banish**, begin at the base and rub toward the top. If it is for **drawing**, begin at the top and rub toward the base. The oil may be poured directly on to the candle. Hold your concentration throughout the process, and seal the candle when finished with the anointing.

When you have finished dressing your candles, extinguish the Altar candles in reverse order of that in which they were lit. Sound the bell three times for dismissal.

Now, clean off the Altar and re-set it, placing all candles in their proper places or holders for the ritual. Be certain that they are quietly undisturbed prior to the time designated for lighting them. If you have any visitors in the meantime, cover the Altar up with a white soft veiling of some sort. It is best not to trust any "Evil-Eye" influence to be cast upon your Altar, possibly causing your spell to abort. Remember that it is your very best friends and closest relatives who are most likely to sneer upon your workings, and cause them to go afowl, even though unintentionally, so it is best to keep your works absolutely secret.

### LIGHTING YOUR CANDLES

Matches on an Altar are Taboo. The reason for this, is they are tipped with phosphorous and sulphur (Brimstone) — elements which release noxious fumes when ignited, and are used in the Black Arts to invoke demonic entities. Striking matches to light candles which have been blessed and charged would therefore seem futile.

There are many customs regarding the lighting procedure, one of the most ancient and charming having been described earlier, and known as "Drawing Down the Sun."

However, beginners in the Art seldom have a permanent Altar with a perpetual flame from which to light their candles, so alternate methods must be used. You will need a lighting taper, or a box or lighting sticks, both available at the candle shop. If you use the lighting sticks, you will also have to have a small candle, usually one of the votive type in a container or glass, to use as a "pilot" lamp.

Light the small candle in another room, from a butane lighter, or natural gas flame, and carry it to your ritual Altar. Then, using the taper or lighting stick, light the other candles from it, in this order: If you have Altar candles, these are always lit first. Next, light any Astral or Personal candles. Last, visualizing your desires, light the Offertory Purpose candle(s).

# SUGGESTED OILS FOR
# CANDLE "CHARGING"

In essence, a "spell" involves the act of projecting one's thoughts, fantasies, and visualizations of desired outcome into the Cosmic Forces, (or) invoking the assistance of higher Entities, and causing them to act, or influence material affairs.

However, just as a medium of transferance is required in order to bring a video image into your home, the same is necessary in order to transfer a thought-image into the Cosmic realm.

One of the classic methods is via the employment of the principle of combustion, by candle-burning.

However, first a "universal fluid condenser," in the form of the oil with which the candle is dressed, is used to transfer the thought-patterns onto the wax, wherein they are firmly "recorded" or embedded. Then, by burning, the ideas are released into Cosmic "fire" or "spirit."

The preparation of universal fluid condensers is a complicated study in itself, requiring much skill and concentration, therefore the average person is better off buying prepared oils of the proper kind, so that a good variety may be kept on hand for the times when they are needed.

Following are a few suggested oils for various uses:

For dressing Altar candles, and memorial candles — "Candle-Dressing"; "Frankincense Oil"; "Frankincense and Myrrh Oil"; "Sandalwood"; "Lotus"; or "Rose."

For drawing something or someone closer to yourself — "Attraction"; "Magnet"; or "Come to Me".

To obtain Peace — "Myrrh Oil."

To obtain Spiritual assistance in difficult circumstances — "Holy Oil"; "Spirit Oil"; or the oils named after specific Saints, or Dieties.

To obtain employment — "Success."

For healing — "Balm of Gilead."

To stimulate mental faculties, pass an examination, etc. — "Mercury Oil"; "Wisteria."

To conquer obstacles or hindrance — "High John the Conqueror"; "7-Power."

To obtain necessary money for fundamentals — "Horn of Plenty."

To obtain "extra" money — "Money-Drawing"; "Gambler's Luck"; "Bayberry."

To bring about Love or sexual relationship — "Love Oil"; "Rose"; or, "Venus Oil" (for true love with marriage in mind) "Jupiter Oil" (for an affair of lust.)

For banishing unwanted influence — "Uncrossing"; "Jinx-removing"; "Holy Oil"; or your personal Zodiac Oil.

For banishing an undesired person — "Exodus."

To protect from bodily harm — "Santa Barbara"; "Saint Michael."

To protect against psychic attack — "Spiritual Protection"; "Lotus"; "Jasmine"; or "Magnolia."

To banish bad entities — "Exorcism Oil."

To break a hex — "Witchbane"; and sometimes "Black Cat."

To change luck from bad to good — "Fast Luck"; "9-Mystery."

To thwart an enemy — "Black Arts"; "Mars Oil"; "Santa Barbara."

To reverse evil sent to you — "Witchbane"; or "Mars Oil."

To confuse another — "Confusion."

To influence another's thoughts — "Compelling"; "Bend-Over Oil."

To control the actions of another — "Controlling."

To force someone to do your bidding — "Commanding."

This is just a small list, and there are hundreds of oils available at different supply houses. Also, there are other ways in which many of the oils are used other than for dressing candles. So consult with your supplier, or a book which goes further into the subject of oils, if you have a special purpose which is not given in this list.

# INCENSE

One of the most ancient customs in Religious and Spiritual practices, is the burning of incense.

It has always been believed that to scent the atmosphere with fine, rare and exotic fragrances will attract the Gods, Angels, and Good Spirits, and repel demons and all manner of evil entities.

Today we know that stimulation of the olfactory nerves (our sense of smell) brings about certain changes in our thinking processes, and emotional responses. In other words — the things you smell affect the way you feel. If you smell onions frying on a grill, or hickory smoke, your brain tells you you are hungry, because the scent has started the flow of your digestive juices. The smell of certain flowers may make you feel sad because they remind you of a funeral parlour.

However, there are certain fragrances which will elevate your feelings of Spirituality, or remind you of Love (often to the point of arrousing passion,) others which make you think of prosperity, or clear your mind of interference so that you might meditate more easily...etc.

Do not be afraid to burn plenty of incense, provided it is good quality, made with wood, resin, or gum bases. The cheap stick or cone incenses imported from Japan or India are often made with dried dung as a base, due to the shortage of woods, resins, or gums of the proper kinds in those areas. Therefore it is heavily perfumed with cheap musks to mask the odor of burning dung. These types of incense are fine to remove obnoxious fumes from your home or car, such as tobacco smoke, or pet smells, bathroom odors, etc. But they have no place on an Altar, or for Spiritual and Occult works.

The Spiritual incenses are compounded from powdered Sandalwood, Eucalyptus, Frankincense, Myrrh, Dragon's Blood, Benzoin, Herbs, Barks, and spices, and flowers. Essential Oils supply much of the fragrance. There are many which are self-burning, and some which must be placed on glowing charcoals especially compounded for Altar use. These charcoals are not made of the same type woods as your briquettes used in the barbecue.

The popular self-burning powdered incenses for Spiritual use will be scented and colored according to the purpose for which they are recommended. The name and color of the incense will tell you what it is best used for, such as red (rose) for love; green (bayberry or evergreen) for money, etc.

When dressing and setting up your Altar candles, pure frankincense, or frankincense with myrrh, or rose, sandalwood or jasmine are recommended.

Then, while charging your purpose candles, and during your meditation or prayer sessions, burn one that is best matched to your intentions.

Incenses may be burned in any type of metal shallow container which is open. Never put a lid on the burner unless you want to smother it out.

If you are burning a resin incense on charcoals, be certain the burner is not placed directly in contact with furniture, or any surface which might be damaged by high heat. Set it up on a trivet, or better still, place a layer of sand or fine gravel in the burner, with a piece of foil in which to place the charcoal. This will insulate it quite well.

It is always a good idea to line your burner with fresh foil each time you use it, whether or not you use charcoals. That way it can be used for various types of incenses without mingling them or contaminating the bottom of your burner with a gummy residue which is nearly impossible to remove.

Some spells call for disposal of all remnants by burying, and you can be certain of gathering all of the ashes from individual spells, if they are contained in foil.

# SEALS AND PARCHMENTS

A very popular custom worth mentioning is the use of "Magic Seals of Power," or handwritten Parchments in conjunction with candle burning.

There are literally hundreds of different seals, in keeping with various traditions, which are available from most supply shops. These are printed on Parchment, and ready for use.

There are Seals of Solomon, used to invoke certain specifically desired influences; Seals of the different Saints, in the Catholic tradition; Seals from the 6th and 7th Books of Moses, in the Mosaic Magical tradition; Veves, which summon various Saints or Spirits, in the Carribbean tradition, etc.

While some of these Seals are intended to be carried upon the person, or concealed in the domicile, most are also used with candle-burning rituals.

The Seal must be anointed with a Spiritual Oil, the petitioner's initials written on the back, and placed underneath the candle while it is burning. At the final meditation or prayer session, and just before the candle goes out, the Seal is ignited from the candle and burned in the incense burner. The ashes are buried with the remnants of the spell.

A very ancient custom, which seems to add power and impetus as well as meaning, is to write one's needs or desires out on a piece of Virgin Parchment paper. This must be paper which has never been re-cycled, or used for any other purpose.

Many use the old traditional sheepskin parchment, whenever it is available, as it bears some resemblance to the symbolic "Sacrificial Lamb." (The same effect may be obtained by rubbing the parchment paper with a piece of lamb fat, or lanolin obtained in the drug store...)

If your spell is for money, write the amount of money you desire on the parchment. If it is a love spell, write, "I (Mary) desire to have (John) fall in love with me.". . .etc. Whatever the purpose of the spell, write it out on the parchment.

This is traditionally written in "Dove's Blood" red ink, with a feather quill pen.

Anoint the edges of the parchment with the oil used to dress your candle, and burn it at the conclusion of the spell, as with the Seals.

Seals may be used along with Parchments, if you would like to use both. The Seals are usually placed under the Astral candles, and in some cases under the Altar candles. The Parchment must always be placed underneath the petition candle.

SEAL OF GREAT GENERATION – For wealth, honor, and promotions.

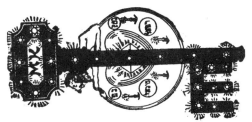

MASTER KEY SEAL – Symbol of health, good fortune, and success.

THIRD PENTACLE OF VENUS – This seal reputedly attracts love.

# PART TWO

## Planning and Timing

# PLANNING

This section of the book is for the student or operator who strives toward perfection. The more you learn of these concepts, the greater degree of success you are likely to achieve.

Good planning saves money and energies expended! "Magic" is like Nature itself — so logically, success in Magic requires working in harmony with Nature, not against it. Therefore, when planning a spell, there are several important factors to consider when determining the best time for the work.

First and foremost, it must be at a time when the operator is likely to be at peak efficiency. So if you are aware of your own "cycles," consider this in your planning.

Keep an Almanac, Astrological Calendar, or Ephemeris which gives the Moon's phases, and the signs through which the Moon is traversing. Study and learn the effects of the different Planetary influences. Refer to the Planetary "Time-Table," and learn to calculate the length of time in each Planetary hour, so that you may time your spells to originate at an hour which will carry the most power for your specific purpose.

Decide on the correct Moon Phase, and the day which carries the Planetary influence you wish to work under.

Know the effects of the Moon in the various Zodiac signs, and check the date you propose for your spell against the sign which the Moon will be in on that day. If it is detrimental, start over, until you have found a date which is astrologically harmonious with your work. Finally, decide whether it is to be a day or night operation, and then decide upon the exact Planetary hour.

If your spell requires that you influence another person, here are some things to consider: There are times in each day which render a person more receptive to the will of another, so learn the person's habits. The more "passive" the target, or recipient, the more vulnerable to suggestibility. A person is **most** receptive to outside or unconscious influence when in a state of "dream sleep," which begins about 5 or 6 hours after falling asleep, and ordinarily continues until he awakens, if he is a "normal" sleeper.

There are other times in each day which are equally fertile periods of suggestibility, if you do not know the sleeping habits. Times when boredom or day-dreaming are most likely (just prior to breaks at work, or quitting time) or at hours when time hangs most heavily (during travel in traffic on a freeway, for instance.)

If the spell is of an immediate need, you will have to settle on a time which may not be the most perfect, or the easiest in which to expedite the particular work. But at least don't choose an impossible day and hour (such as Mars for a spell of love or peace and harmony.) Nature's balance-factor is too heavily weighed against you to expect good results.

the goal is of major proportions (like desired matrimony, the quisition of real or personal property, a promotion, a legal ecision, etc.) it is much better to wait — even several weeks or months, if necessary, to set the exact date and time for the most positive results. Anything really worth having, is worth waiting for. You cannot pick peaches from the tree in midwinter! There is a perfect time for everything — just learn to work **with** Nature, and She will provide for all your desires and needs.

If you are trying to help someone else, timing is most important of all, as "Sympathetic" magic is the most difficult, except in cases where you are very closely associated with the person for whom you are doing the spell. Otherwise, you must be able to personally "assume" the person's problems as though they were your own, while not allowing them to actually affect you physically, or remain latent in your subconscious, causing you emotional upset.

### RENEWAL

Many spells have to be renewed, or repeated from time to time if you wish the effects to be permanent. The "permanent" effect is one which must mature, such as spells for domestic love or faithfullness, the desire to be a successful business person, the desire for thriving health, etc.

Few, if any spells last forever, without working at it. Conditions are constantly modified by changing planetary positions, and eventually they either cease altogether, or, in some instances, may reverse their action, unless the operation is renewed. Don't be like the husband who showers his lady-love with attention and gifts, whispering "I love you" a thousand times prior to marriage, then once his goal is achieved rarely remembers her birthday, let alone the magic words he spoke during courtship. You can be sure the spell wears off!

For truly sustained effects, repeat the operation at least quarterly — and never fail to thank the Spirits. It is also good to now and then burn a devotional candle dedicated to your favorite Diety, just out of thanksgiving for guidance and inspiration. This practice keeps you from slipping into a materialistic state of egomania regarding your magic, and by so, diminishing your personal powers. It is good to remember that you communicate with the Spirits Spiritually, not materially, or physically. Letters to Santa Claus are an illusion and deception! But if the child "sees" old Santa in his sled, sailing over the sky — a "Miraculous" intervention just might grant his deepest wish — by **some** means!

# THE PLANETARY HOURS

The "Planetary hours" are a different concept from "time."

The length of each "hour" is not determined by a time clock. They may be co-ordinated with regular time as a convenient reference, but must not be confused.

They indicate the prevalence of one of the various types of "influence" or Psychic tides at any given time.

The length of each "hour" in the days and nights change, according to the seasons. In the summer, the "hours" in each day are longer than the "hours" in the nights. In the winter it is reversed. That is to say, that each of the seven influences will prevail for more or less than 60 minutes at a time, in its cyclic manifestation, or appearance.

This may be determined by consulting an almanac which gives the exact length of days and nights (Old Farmer's Almanac.) Otherwise, you must obtain the times of Sunrise and Sunset from the newspaper, weather bureau, etc. The length of time (in minutes) between Sunset and Sunrise the following day, divided by 12, will indicate the number of minutes in each Planetary hour of the night.

"Midday" and "Midnight" will always be exactly half-way between, disregarding the terms "Noon" and "Midnight" as we consider them normally.

The dividing-line between two different Planetary hours, when the change-over is taking effect, is referred to as a "cusp."

Just as the fisherman must consider the tides of lakes and oceans for his advantage, so must the magician consider the "psychic tides" when planning his works.

**TO CALCULATE THE PLANETARY HOURS:** If you do not have the table of Planetary hours handy, and forget their order of rotation, here is a way in which you can make the calculation. (See illustration of wheel.)

First, draw a 7-pointed star, in one continuous line, starting at the top. Then, taking the points in the order in which they were drawn, label them with the Planetary attributes according to the order of the day of the week, that is, Sun., Mon., Tues., Wed., etc.

The order of the Planetary hour succession rotates in an East-to-West progression, around the circumference of the circle of points.

Sunrise each day inaugurates the first hour of the day, which is characteristic of that particular day of the week and named the same. Therefore, for instance, the first hour on Sunday would be an hour of the Sun; 2nd-Venus; 3rd-Mercury; 4th-Moon; 5th-Saturn; 6th-Jupiter; and 7th-Mars. On Monday the first hour is a Moon hour; on Tuesday the first is a Mars hour, etc., always following the same order of rotation.

# WHEEL OF ROTATION OF
# THE PLANETARY HOURS

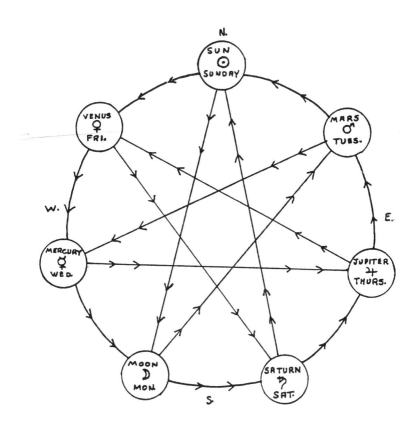

# TABLE OF PLANETARY HOURS

| Marker | Hour of the Day | SUN ☉ | MON ☽ | TUES ♂ | WED ☿ | THURS ♃ | FRI ♀ | SAT ♄ |
|---|---|---|---|---|---|---|---|---|
| SUNRISE | 1ST | SUN | MOON | MARS | MERCURY | JUPITER | VENUS | SATURN |
|  | 2ND | VENUS | SATURN | SUN | MOON | MARS | MERCURY | JUPITER |
|  | 3RD | MERCURY | JUPITER | VENUS | SATURN | SUN | MOON | MARS |
|  | 4TH | MOON | MARS | MERCURY | JUPITER | VENUS | SATURN | SUN |
|  | 5TH | SATURN | SUN | MOON | MARS | MERCURY | JUPITER | VENUS |
| MIDDAY | 6TH | JUPITER | VENUS | SATURN | SUN | MOON | MARS | MERCURY |
|  | 7TH | MARS | MERCURY | JUPITER | VENUS | SATURN | SUN | MOON |
|  | 8TH | SUN | MOON | MARS | MERCURY | JUPITER | VENUS | SATURN |
|  | 9TH | VENUS | SATURN | SUN | MOON | MARS | MERCURY | JUPITER |
|  | 10TH | MERCURY | JUPITER | VENUS | SATURN | SUN | MOON | MARS |
|  | 11TH | MOON | MARS | MERCURY | JUPITER | VENUS | SATURN | SUN |
| VESPER | 12TH | SATURN | SUN | MOON | MARS | MERCURY | JUPITER | VENUS |

| Marker | Hour of the Night | SUN ☉ | MON ☽ | TUES ♂ | WED ☿ | THURS ♃ | FRI ♀ | SAT ♄ |
|---|---|---|---|---|---|---|---|---|
| SUNSET | 1ST | JUPITER | VENUS | SATURN | SUN | MOON | MARS | MERCURY |
| TWILIGHT | 2ND | MARS | MERCURY | JUPITER | VENUS | SATURN | SUN | MOON |
| NIGHTFALL | 3RD | SUN | MOON | MARS | MERCURY | JUPITER | VENUS | SATURN |
|  | 4TH | VENUS | SATURN | SUN | MOON | MARS | MERCURY | JUPITER |
|  | 5TH | MERCURY | JUPITER | VENUS | SATURN | SUN | MOON | MARS |
| MIDNIGHT | 6TH | MOON | MARS | MERCURY | JUPITER | VENUS | SATURN | SUN |
|  | 7TH | SATURN | SUN | MOON | MARS | MERCURY | JUPITER | VENUS |
|  | 8TH | JUPITER | VENUS | SATURN | SUN | MOON | MARS | MERCURY |
|  | 9TH | MARS | MERCURY | JUPITER | VENUS | SATURN | SUN | MOON |
|  | 10TH | SUN | MOON | MARS | MERCURY | JUPITER | VENUS | SATURN |
|  | 11TH | VENUS | SATURN | SUN | MOON | MARS | MERCURY | JUPITER |
|  | 12TH | MERCURY | JUPITER | VENUS | SATURN | SUN | MOON | MARS |

# THE NATURE OF THE PLANETARY INFLUENCES

There are seven different types of influences, or psychic tides, which ebb and flow at intervals, in much the same way as the ocean's tides ebb and flow with the motion of the Moon. These pyschic tides affect the way which we feel, think, and often our actions. The atmosphere will seem to be charged with a particular idea during each cycle. The days of the week, and the Planetary hours are named according to the ancient God or Goddess who represented that department of life. Your activities should be planned according to the power which is most prevalent at the particular time — day and hour, if you would make most advantageous use of the energies that Nature provides.

## SUN

The days and hours of the Sun impart an influence favorable to acts related to **active vitality**. During an eclipse of the Sun, nothing must be undertaken in the realm or magic, as it is an unfortunate time and things fail therein.

Spells are initiated at the Sun hour to bring swift success, fast luck, new money, instant action, etc.

The beneficial currents of "Sun power" are ideal for activities dealing with advancement of position, political influence, self-aggrandizement, theatrical success and glory, promotional schemes, and release from captivity.

The Sun hours are ideal for meditation upon Spiritual cleansing and revitalization.

## MOON

The days and hours of the Moon are most favorable to acts related to **vegetative activity** — security, fore-knowledge, journeys.

The Moon **reflects, inspires, and energizes emotions.**

Moon hours are good for casting spells for romance, sexual pursuits, etc., and for the desire to travel for pleasure.

The Moon's effect is also hypnotic, and lends an influence which inclines toward vulnerability, therefore rendering the weak or uninformed open to attack, and capable of being wounded or controlled by another.

# MARS

Mars is the **motivator.** It has powerful positive and negative influences, and is a force to be considered with utmost caution.

Mars does not know nor care about "right" or "wrong." It only strives after **victory.** It incites courage, bravery, and vindictiveness. It is inclined toward **combativeness**, and its power favors domination, politics, athletics, surgery, industry, difficulties in lawsuits, etc. It seems to furnish the necessary drive and force required to **conquer** or **win.**

Martian influence is a **protector** par excellence, and the Mars hour is useful for petitions of protection against enemies, the "Evil Eye" and demonic attack or possession.

It is also the time to launch an all-out attack on an enemy or adversary. But remember — a Martian-type spell is not for the squeamish or half-hearted. It is like the Gladiator — it will drive to the **kill** if uncontrolled, and is very likely to leave a trail of blood in its wake!

Therefore, if it is only desired to thwart, or inhibit another's actions, without actually hurting the person, then Saturn is the influence to utilize. Always carefully consider the Karmic aspects of a Martian spell, and remember, one is entitled only to **like kind** of retribution — **no more!!** Any "overdraught" will be subject to The Law of Three!

In **controlling** the Martian influence, you must learn to modify it with other Planetary or Zodiacal influences. For instance, use a day of Mercury or Venus, with a Mars hour, and the Moon in an Air sign, to combat injustice for a favorable outcome (during New Moon — 1st quarter.)

The Mars-Sun cusp is the time to seek paroles or liberation, whether deserved or not. The spell cast to obtain freedom is well-timed if the power can be released at the precise moment of the cusp, with the Moon in a Fire sign. For peaceful separations or hand-partings, choose a day of Venus, Moon full-to-waning in an Earth sign, with the Mars-Sun influence.

The Jupiter-Mars cusp is good for psycho-kinetic magic (mind over matter) — change the weather, divert storms, influence gaming devices to win, and to bring about "miraculous" (spontaneous) healings, etc...with the Sun in an Air sign, the Moon in a water sign.

## MERCURY

Mercury is "the manipulator." Its influence is favorable to all acts requiring **adaptiveness** — skills, commerce; medicine, diplomacy, counseling, changes, etc.

Mercury hours lend themselves adeptly to mental feats of all kinds, or to works aimed at bending the mind of another.

Use the Mercury hours to cast spells aimed at bringing about quick changes of all kinds, but it will work best when the Moon is in a mutable sign. If it is in a cardinal or fixed sign the work could fail and result in frustration or confusion.

To change bad luck to good, use a Mercury hour on a day of Venus. This is **not** for the chronically greedy, or the malcontent, as if they are actually enjoying their due share of good luck but simply don't take advantage of the benefits or make good use of them — the result could turn the tables and bring them the opposite, in order to teach a lesson.

Remember, Venus leans toward Natural Order, and wants to right things which are wrong or inequitable, and Mercury maneuvers the change. This is also a good time for healing works, when the Moon is in Taurus, Virgo, or Capricorn.

Use a Mercury hour to seek forgiveness, and to make amends, when a strong change in attitudes is desired, or to cause people who have been feuding to make up and become friends. Also to cause troublesome in-laws or relatives to alter their ways, or become reasonable.

When the Moon is in conjunction with Uranus (that is, in the same sign) the Mercury hour is used to completely upset or wreck an establishment or trend.

## JUPITER

The Jupiter influence is predominantly joviality, and is favorable to all acts of sociability, dealings with family, opportunity, group enterprise, civic functions, etc.

Jupiter's effect is one of **expansion**. This is a concept which often misleads most into believing that everything about it is **good**. Remember, Jupiter brings **more** — abundance! But it is more of the same as that which exists, not something different. It does not activate change. Therefore to invoke Jupiter on behalf of someone who is already suffering, or lacking, would bring about total despair or poverty. It's the influence under which "the rich get richer and the poor get poorer," so use caution. It will bring a bumper crop if the seeds have been properly sown, and the field well tended; but it won't grow hair on a billiard ball — only a nice shine.

Jupiter's influence would be good to put a "fat" spell on an individual who is egotistically and obnoxiously vain about his or her slender physique. It would certainly teach a little tolerance and sympathy for those not so fortunately blessed.

When someone is inclined to become fettered with the accumulation of too much of anything, a **banishing** ritual may be performed to rid them of the prevalence of the Jupiter influence. This must be done with the Moon waning in Capricorn, Gemini, or Virgo.

Jupiter hours are good for spells to increase Male fertility in humans or animals. For more verility use the Jupiter-Mars cusp.

Jupiter hours are good for turning a good business into a "bonanza," or to achieve a raise in salary or promotion. Also for matters of family re-union.

Cast spells for "increase" during the Jupiter hours. But remember, there has to be something existing to increase. So if it is a money spell, use a dollar bill, or bank book (never depleted) for a "target" or "seed." If the desired increase is for physical strength or stamina, move the time closer to the Jupiter-Mars cusp. The Moon must be waxing in an Earth sign for any increase.

Jupiter is used from winter solstice to vernal equinox for Power, Luck, Glory, Success, and things the Sun is used for ordinarily, as the Sun's power is weaker during this time.

## VENUS
Venus encourages the **Natural** order of things, to protect Nature's balance.

The Venus days and hours are very favorable to anything related to physical perfection and harmony.

While Venus has been regarded as the ideal power for Love spells, this is a haphazard generalization, and must be given further consideration. Remember, Venus guards the Natural order of things, so if the love desired does not in any way disrupt, or corrupt an existing family entity, and if the individuals have already known one another, are favorably matched, and simply need a little "boost" to encourage a true love to manifest and flourish — then Venus is the best influence to utilize for such a love spell.

Also to be considered is the fertility aspect. If the person desiring to obtain the love of another is not serious to the extent of also being willing to assume the responsibility for home and family — that is to say, if only an affair of passion is what is really wanted — the result could by totally disastrous — unwanted pregnancy, a jealous and vindictive lover who is difficult to get loose from, etc.

For such spells of attraction or romantic fascination, it is best to forget the Venus influence until such time as it is desired to make the union permanent, or binding. Meanwhile, use the Mercury (mind-bending manipulator) and Moon (fascination) influences, the Moon being ideal for romantic and emotional vulnerability.

Venus hours are fine to cast spells for fertility — of plants, animals, or humans, also corporate entities. Also to bring peace in the home, average good luck that has been lacking, anything dealing with music, arts and crafts, home economics, and beauty.

## SATURN

Saturn's influence is "crystallization." It slows down, thwarts, restricts, limits according to Natural Law. It is favorable to acts related to longevity, the abstract, the unknown, and Law.

Saturn's days and hours are ideal for finding lost objects, or stolen goods, making someone reveal secrets or hidden knowledge (for benevolent purposes) and achieving quite "impossible" feats designed to bestow honor and dignity.

Take advantage of Saturn hours for meditations to obtain wisdom, for self-control (ridding one of undesired habits,) or to lower the blood pressure or pulse-rate.

When the Moon wanes in Scorpio, the Saturn influence is good for casting spells to bind, thwart, or cause someone to cease and desist from a particular action, and to "freeze" someone or something in a present condition or state. This could result in the arrest of a progressive disease. (This spell would have to be re-inforced under the Sun-Venus influence.)

Saturn hours favor the collection of debts. Cast spells at this time, when the Moon is in an Earth sign, to reap benefits and rewards from efforts expended, or to obtain needed relief from want.

The Saturn-Jupiter cusp, with Moon in Taurus, is the ideal time for peace making. This cusp favors benevolent leadership, practical idealism, brotherly love, selflessness, and philanthropic acts. So use this time to "help" in any way, and it will bring an appropriate Spiritual reward.

Always keep in mind — Saturn's influence is **practical, saving** and **beneficial, not** "evil". It is best left alone by those with evil designs.

# THE MOON IN SPELLCASTING

Lunar terms:

**FIRST QUARTER** (Waxing): Right portion of the Moon is illuminated.

**FULL MOON:** Moon reaches exact opposition to the Sun. Total illumination.

**LAST QUARTER** (Waning): Left portion of the Moon is illuminated.

**NEW MOON:** Sun and Moon are in conjunction. Total darkness.

\* \* \* \*

The Moon is a sign-post which indicates the prevailing direction of the Life-force, the reproductive energy that animates all living things — plant, animal, or humans.

When the Moon is waxing, Life energy on Earth increases. When the Moon is waning, Life energy is decreasing.

The waxing phase is used to activate, vitalize, or increase. The waning phase is utilized to banish, or decrease.

For spells of a nature in which it is desired to gain or build up something (Love, money, popularity, acquisition of a job or position, etc.) the spell must be done during the Moon's waxing phase — from New to Full.

For spells of a banishing nature (to get rid of a certain illness or disease, an undesirable neighbor you wish to have move away, a lawsuit you wish to have dismissed, etc.) the spell must be done during the Moon's waning period — from Full to dark.

To bring something into being, begin at the New Moon. To cause the opposite, begin at the Full Moon.

\* \* \* \*

The Moon has a different effect at different times, depending upon the Zodiac sign in which it is traversing.

Its Life-giving force is influenced by the Planets ruling the sign Astrologically.

Its vitality is either boosted, thwarted, or stalemated, and channeled into specific areas of life (or away from them) — all depending upon its position in the heavens.

These positions can be determined by consulting an Astrological calendar, almanac, or ephemeris.

Learn the effects of the Moon in each sign prior to scheduling any important magical works.

## THE MOON IN ARIES

Aries is the "Cardinal" **Fire** sign, which means that it is energetic, innovating, creative, and spirited.

A time filled with enthusiasm, and very favorable for beginnings, and for making changes.

The Moon waning in Aries is excellent for banishing rituals and exorcisms, as the Moon in Aries favors works requiring the skillful wielding of tools or weapons.

Begin your 7-day Novenas during this transit, to obtain something new, or to get rid of an undesired influence, according to the Moon's phase.

During the very middle of the transit, light a candle to seek inspiration for a direction.

Toward the end of the transit, as the Moon draws neerer to Taurus, begin a 7-day Novena for Peace in the Home or place of work.

## THE MOON IN TAURUS

Taurus is the "Fixed" Earth sign, which means it is stable, practical, protective, and materialistic.

Light your 7-day Novena candle for protection at this time.

A bad time to light candles for obtaining anything new. Also a poor time to try to change anything, as the power is on the side of the established position. So if you are considering burning a separation candle, do not do it at this time.

This is also a very bad time for money spells of an immediate need, as those who have the money are deaf to your pleas at this time.

During the last part of the Moon's transit through Taurus things are more favorable for communications and thoughts in practical matters, so you can begin a 7-day candle to obtain necessary money.

## THE MOON IN GEMINI

Gemini is the "Mutable" Air sign, which means that it fluctuates between active-passive in matters pertaining to the mind-intellect.

This is an excellent time to prepare your works, and do your calculations, as it is primarily mental. This is the best possible time for charging your candles, as your powers of mental creativity are at their peak.

Toward the end of the transit, as the Moon approaches Cancer, the trend is more toward emotionalism. This is an ideal time to try to bring about reconcilliations between lovers, or family members who have been at odds.
\* \* \* \*

## THE MOON IN CANCER

Cancer is the "Cardinal" Water sign, which means that it is energetic, innovating, and emotional.

Cast your spell for domination, compelling, or controlling during the Cancer Moon, as power rises sharply to sway or influence others who are easily influenced.

Toward the end of the transit, if the Moon is waxing, light your candles to bring about advancement in position, or to obtain jobs dealing with people.
\* \* \* \*

## THE MOON IN LEO

Leo is the "Fixed" Fire sign, which means that it is aggressive, stable, creative, unchangeable.

Pride is the Leonine attribute, with showmanship being very favored. Now is the time to "perform" your super-flamboyant ritual — many candles, musical background, elegant robes, whatever! If you want to impress someone, "let it all hang out" during the Leonine Moon.

This is the time to cast spells for money, when the money must be obtained from someone else, rather than from capital gains sources.

Love spells are favored during this time also, as the Moon in Leo is excellent for romantic pursuits.

Cast your spell to win a lawsuit, if you know that your case is honest and deserving. However, it would be difficult to attempt to sway a Judge's steadfast ideals if you are in any way at fault, and he will turn against you.

Toward the end of the transit, if the Moon is waxing, cast the spell for promotion or a raise in salary. Light the orange candle for Success!

**** 

## THE MOON IN VIRGO

Virgo is the "Mutable" Earth sign, meaning that it is fluctuating between active and passive. It is protective and materialistic.

Cast your spell for additional money for the home at this time.

Also burn your candles for healing of people or animals.

Moon in Virgo is a good time to dress your candles.

Toward the end of the transit, as the Moon draws toward Libra, cast your spells for compelling, or controlling the actions of another. Also good for spells of romantic conquest, if the Moon is waxing.

****

## THE MOON IN LIBRA

Libra is the "Cardinal" Air sign, which means that it is innovative, inventive and intellectual.

A perfect time to beautify your Temple, make robes, Altar cloths, candles, etc.

If the Moon is waning, you may light a candle to bring about separations, or to break or dissolve any partnership or union. If the Moon is waxing, do the same to bring about or form a partnership or union.

Prepare a special candle dedicated to your favorite Diety or Saint. Now is the time to invoke any assistance in difficult cases.

The waxing Moon in Libra is very favorable to teamwork and joint efforts. Therefore this is the time to seek or accept assistance or collaboration. Often, more than one person meditating upon a project will bring dramatic results.

****

## THE MOON IN SCORPIO

Scorpio is the "Fixed" Water sign, which means that it is stable, unchangeable, and emotional.

This time is only good for planning or devising your secret spells, but do not attempt to enact them now, as the "victim" will fight back and thwart the scheme. So be sure to carefully check out the vulnerability of the object of your spell, and consider his strengths and weaknesses, then calculate the best time for attack! If the odds are in his favor, "let sleeping dogs lie."

If the Moon is full, or approaching fullness, don't rock the boat!

Light a pink candle to keep your love stable, and to bring happiness into the home.

## THE MOON IN SAGITTARIUS

Sagittarius is the "Mutable" Fire sign, which means that it fluctuates between optimism and pessimism, is creative and aggressive.

Schedule your rituals for self-improvement, and to accomplish high ideals at this time.

Do your spells for increase and expansion, if the Moon is waxing.

Also burn your candle for obtaining your Degree from a School of higher learning, or to be accepted into a University, etc.

## THE MOON IN CAPRICORN

Capricorn is the "Cardinal" Earth sign, which means that it is the most materialistic of all the signs. It is innovative, energetic, and practical.

Cast spells for needed money, and it may be forthcoming from surprisingly unexpected sources. Likewise it is the proper time to seek any kind of material necessities, especially if they are long overdue.

If you are seeking revenge on someone, be very cautious, and don't over do it, as Saturn (whose home is Capricorn) guards the non-offender. Do not initiate any injustice, or cruelty, or you will suffer drastic consequences.

# THE MOON IN AQUARIUS

Aquarius is the "Fixed" Air sign, which means that it is concerned with mental and intellectual activity, it is stable, unchangeable.

This time is favorable to anything new and different, therefore it is an ideal time to initiate works that are innovative and revolutionary. But be sure to consider the long-term effects of your expected results before undertaking the work, as you would not benefit in the long run if your achievement were another "Hiroshima." If you are seeking to persuade your husband to abandon the little apartment and buy a home, consider all of the maintenance responsibilities, and the bondage to a long-term mortgage, with rising costs of taxes and insurance, etc.

This is an excellent time for working out the timing of your contemplated spell. The more exacting and "scientifically" it is calculated, the more impetus it will have on your consciousness, and probably bring dramatic results.

The Moon in Aquarius is ideal for engaging in the practice of E.S.P. and Psychic development. So schedule your meditations and practices along this line during the transit.

## THE MOON IN PISCES

Pisces is the "Mutable" Water sign, which means that it is erratic, deceptive, and highly emotional.

This is an ideal time to cast spells aimed specifically at confusion, or throwing an enemy off the track.

It is the best time for retreat and contemplation, or just plain **rest**!

If you are a Spiritual Advisor or Reader, this time will result in your having to listen to long drawn-out sob stories of those feeling sorry for themselves, putting a drain on your own psychic energies. This is, in other words, the time to beware of "Psychic vampires!"

The Moon in Pisces is an excellent time for entertainments or amusements of an escapist nature, especially the fantastic. So, rather than trying to concentrate on an important spell which requires a positive attitude, buy a ticket to Disneyland instead, and schedule the work at a different time.